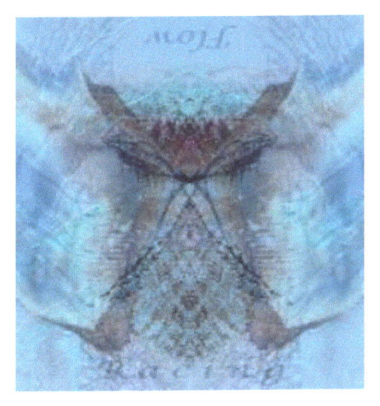

Flow
Racing

I0485160

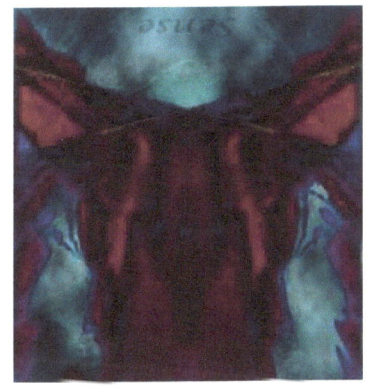

Sense
Grateful

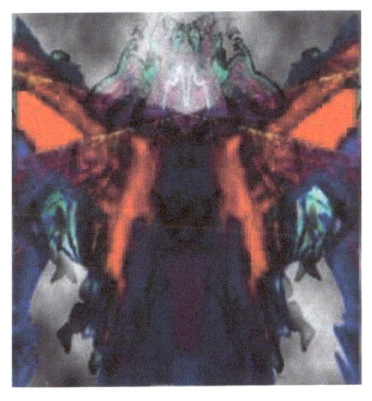

Drive
Movement

3

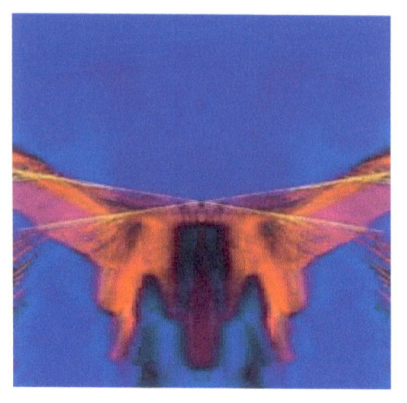

Look
Stand

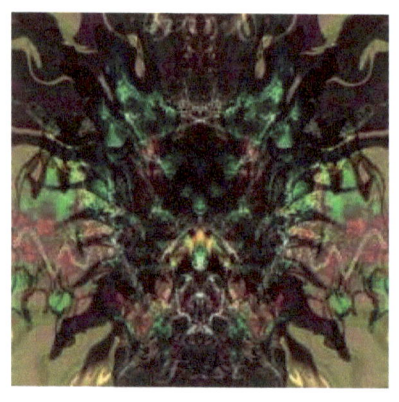

Wade
Fast

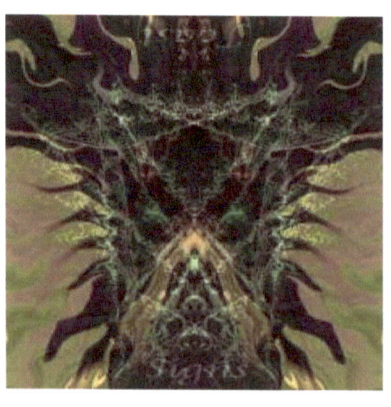

Feast
Signs

4

Take the Healing Energy from these cards to help you succeed in moving forward past whatever is blocking you. Let the energy that comes from the words and the picture move through you and around you as you find the answers that can be yours. The Colors that are here give you many things that can heal you emotionally/physically/spiritually. No matter what you may need let these give you what is Within you for your highest good.

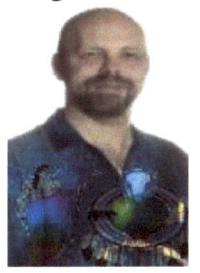

About the Author

Rich CrystalWolfe Baker

My digital artwork has many layers to them since they are being pulled from deep within the spiritual realm to be transferred to paper for people to see and enjoy. I have been doing this for many years. I have been following my inner voice to create from within. This art form gives me the ability to express myself and share with those around me. I thank my friends for giving me the encouragement to listen to my inner voice. Thank you for the chance to share this part of me.

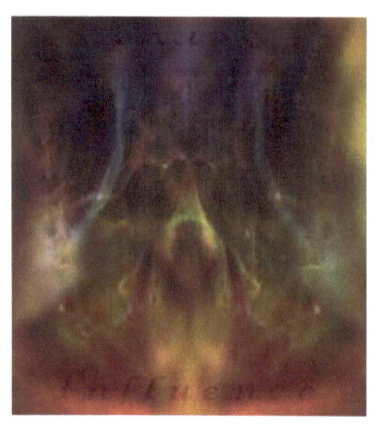

Serve
Influence

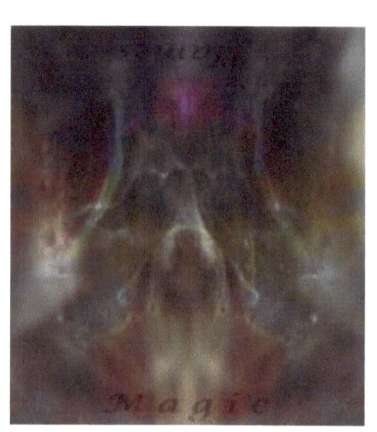

Flames
Magic

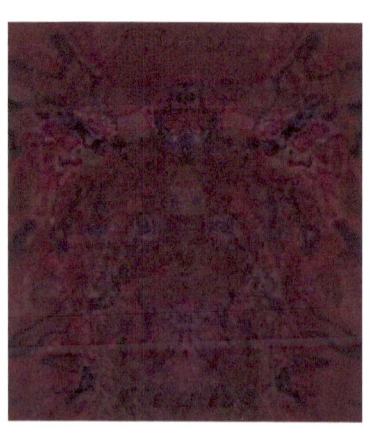

Energy
Light

2

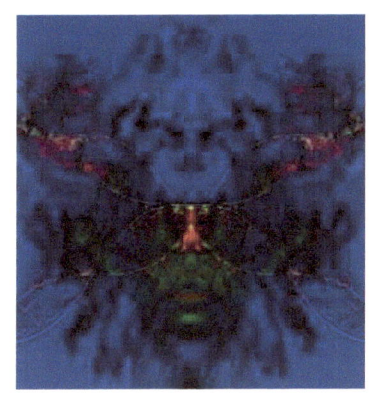

Get
Brought

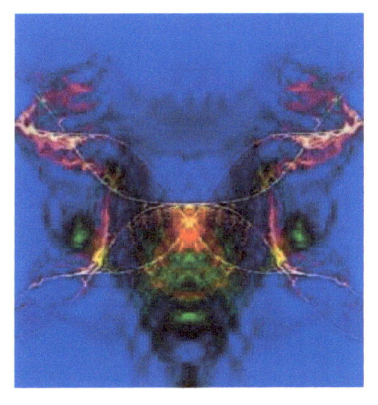

Admit
Take

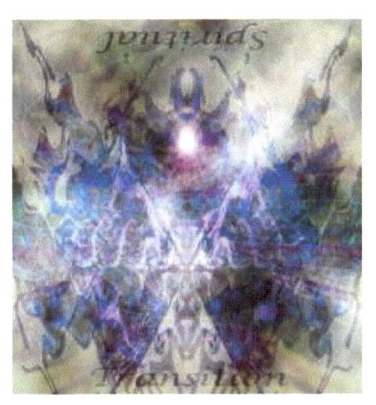

Spiritual
Transition

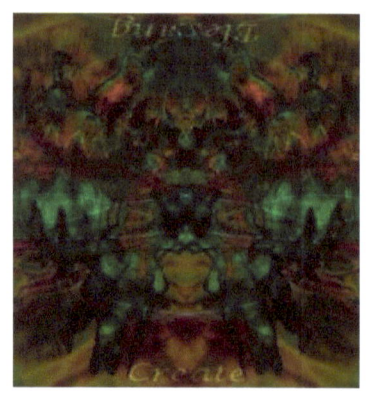

Blessing
Create

Adapt
Sacred

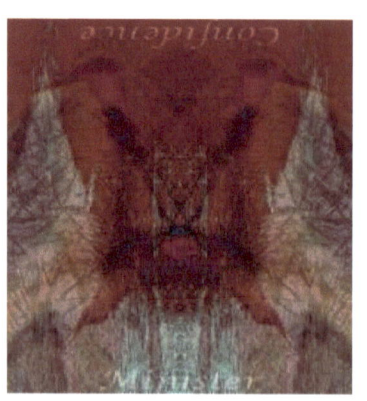

Confidence
Minister

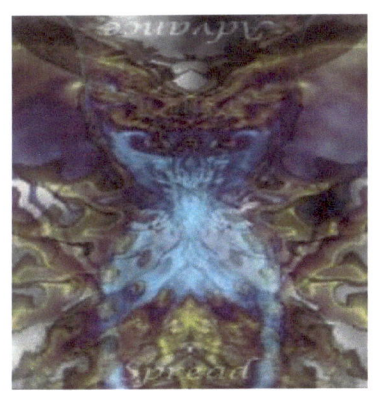

Advance
Spread

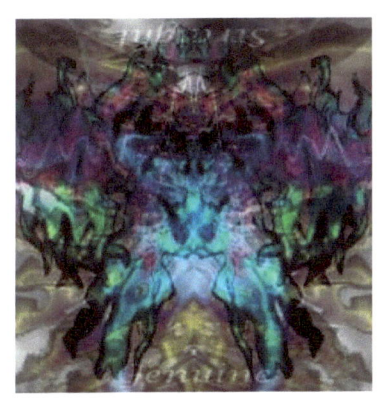

Straight
Genuine

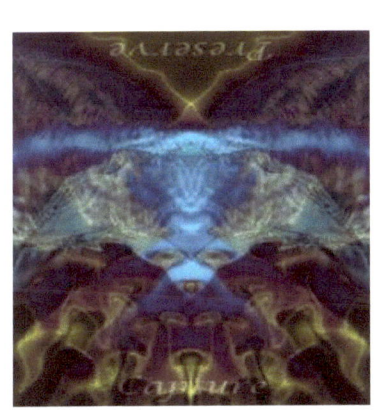

Preserve
Capture

7

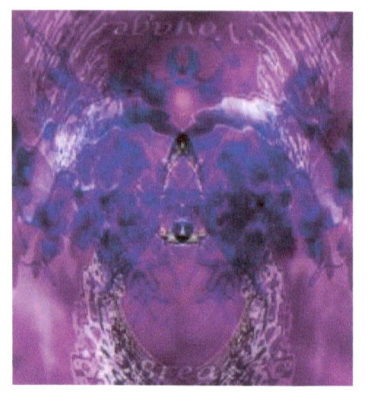

Voyage
Break

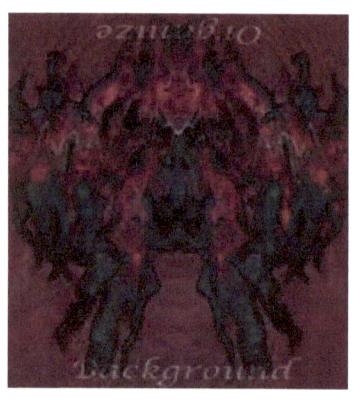

Organize
Background

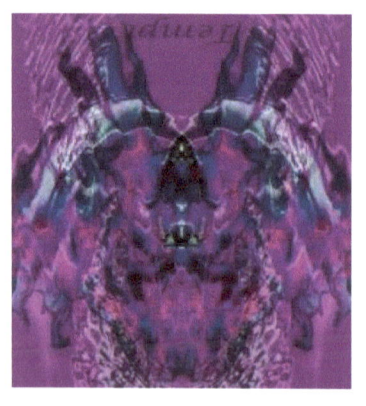

Tempt
Contribute

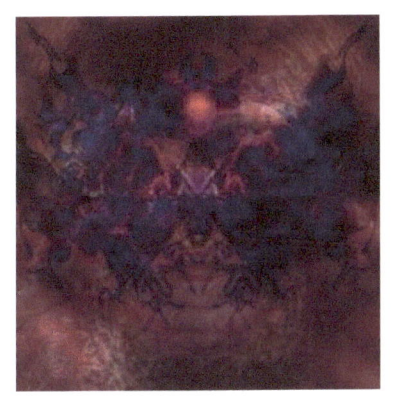

Conquer
Badge

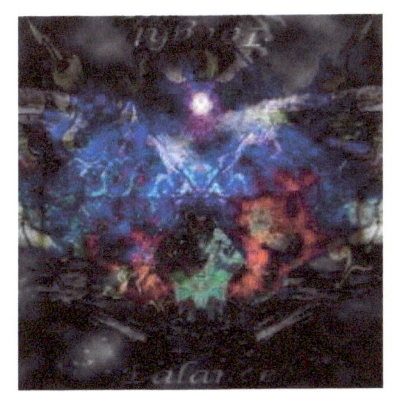

Taught
Balance

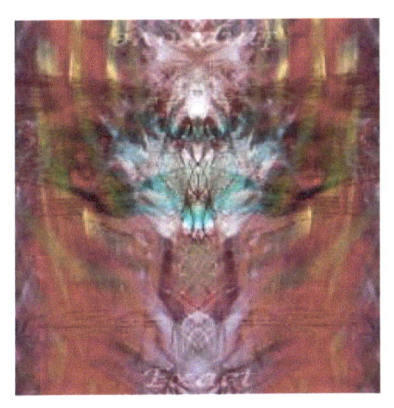

Improve
Exact

9

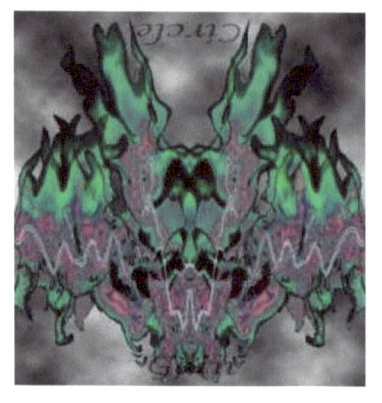

Circle
Gain

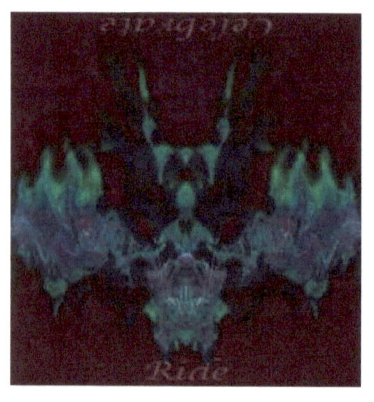

Celebrate
Ride

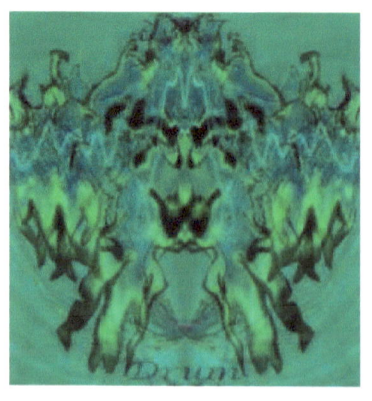

Luck
Drum

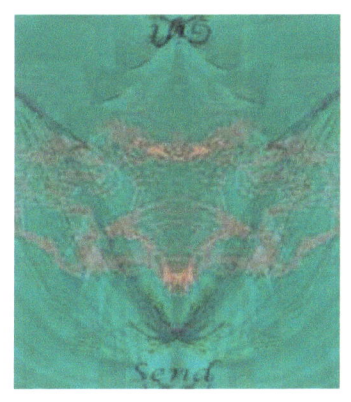

Gift
Send

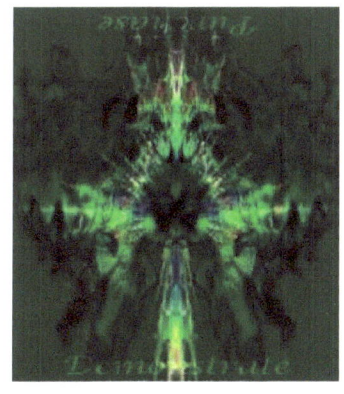

Purchase
Demonstrate

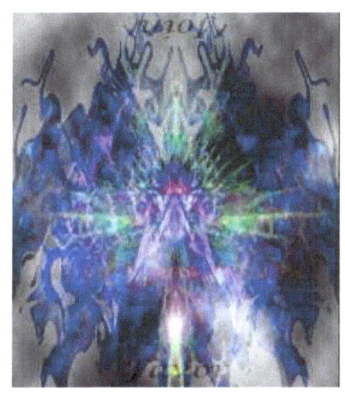

Join
Favor

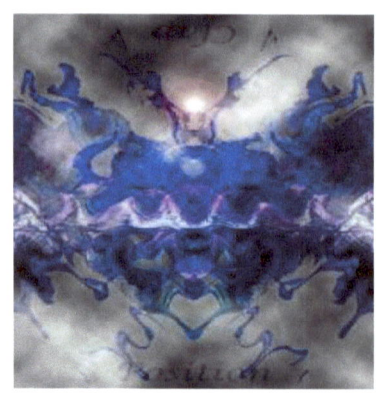

Clap
Position

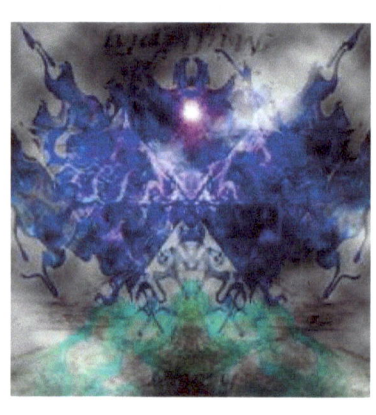

Multiply
Lazy

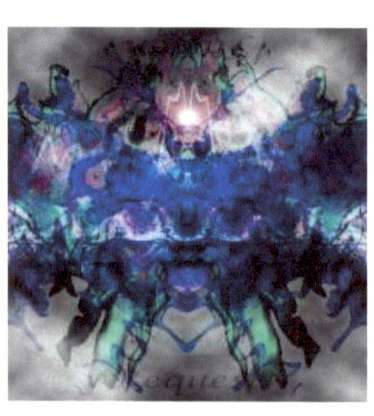

Fasten
Request

12

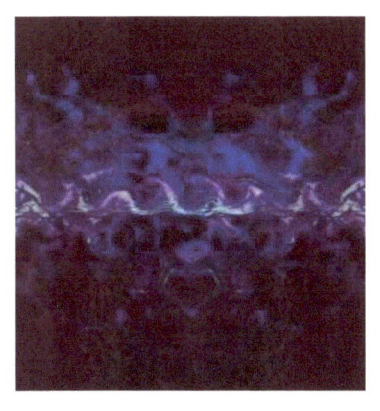

Collect
Rescue

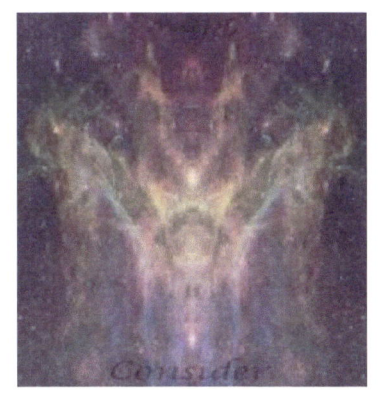

Plow
Consider

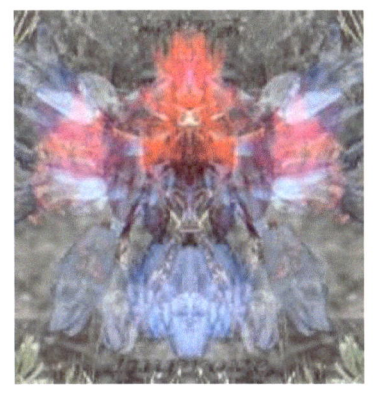

Eager
Improve

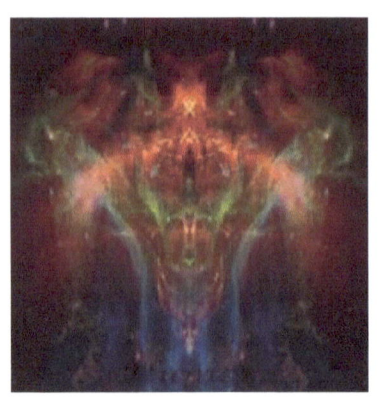

Chance
Humor

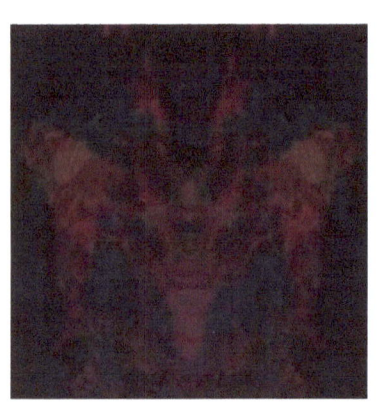

Blend
Feel

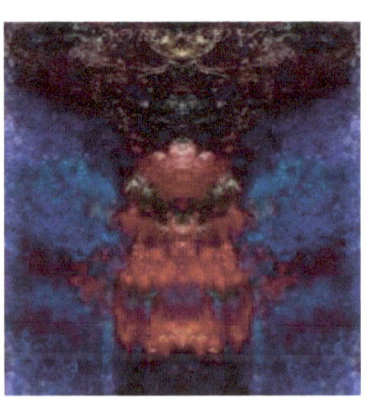

Advance
Repeat

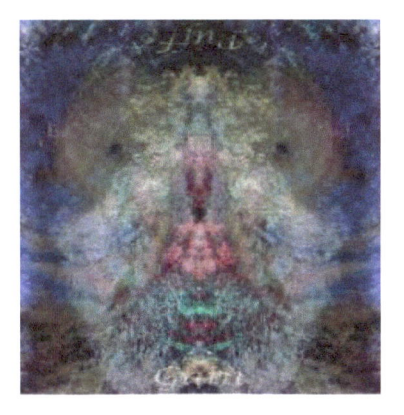

Puff
Gain

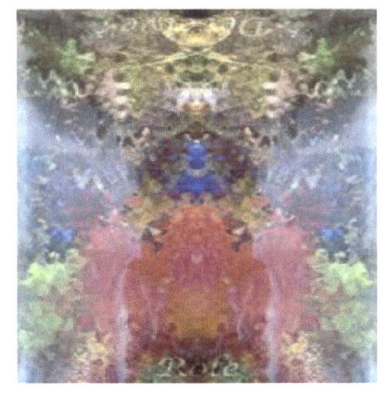

Deceive
Role

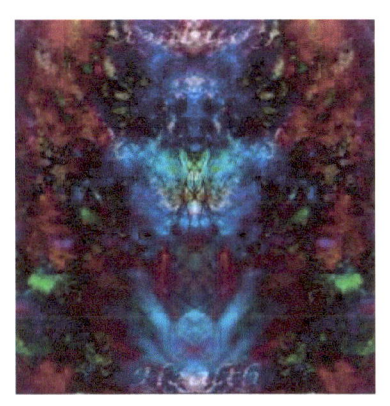

Conquer
Health

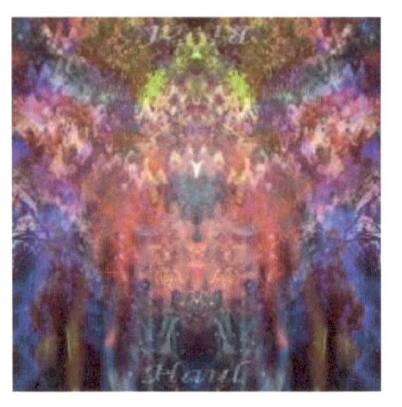

Rival
Haul

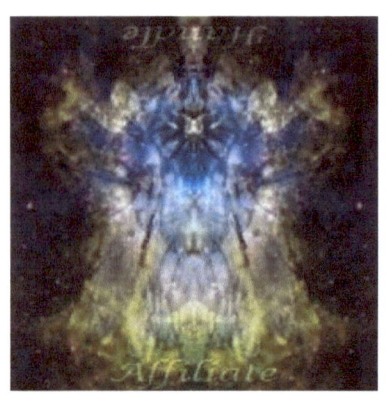

Handle
Affiliate

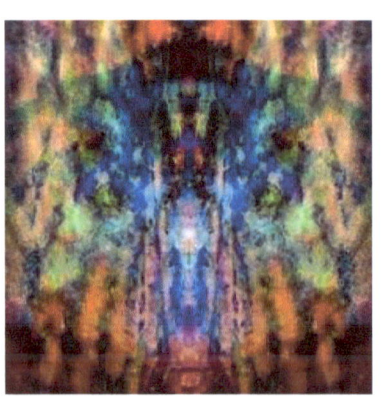

Feel
Fire

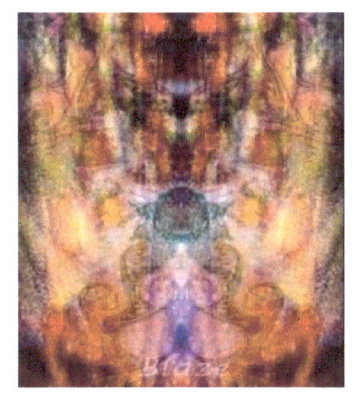

Path
Blaze

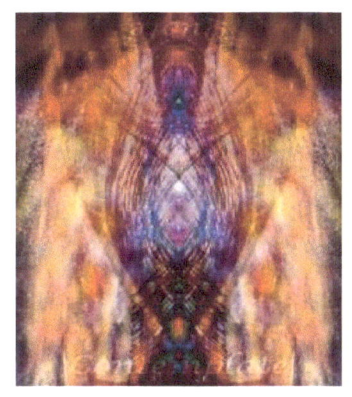

Quote
Contemplate

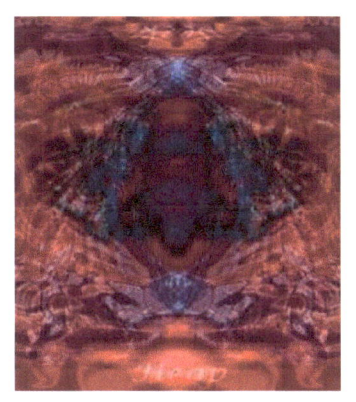

Seek
Heap

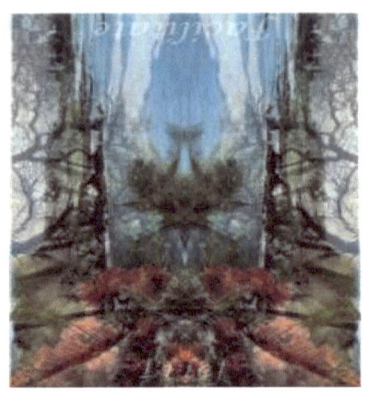

Facilitate
Brief

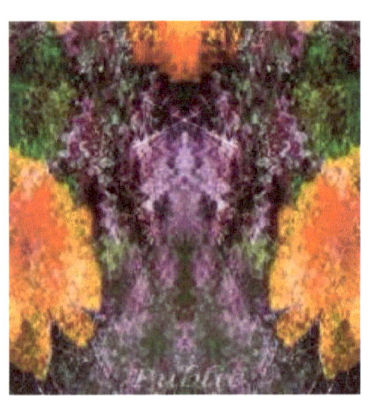

Illustrate
Public

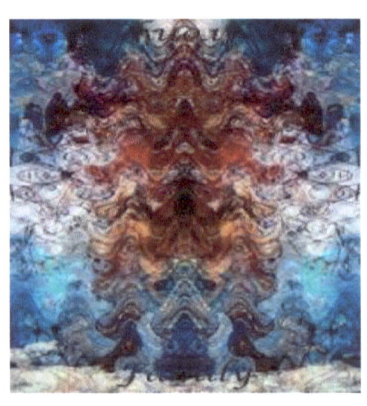

Irony
Family

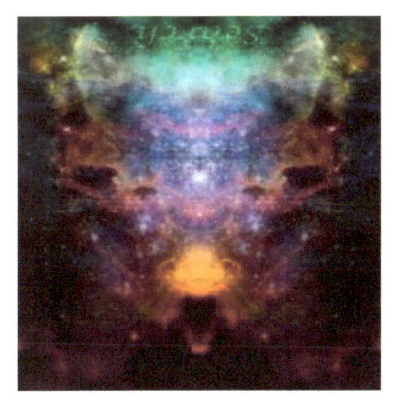

Search
Brief

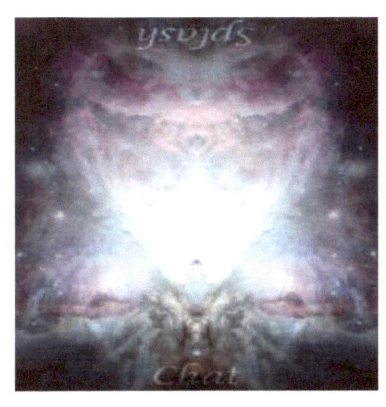

Splash
Chat

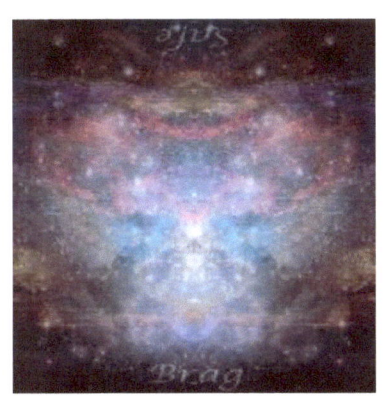

Safe
Brag

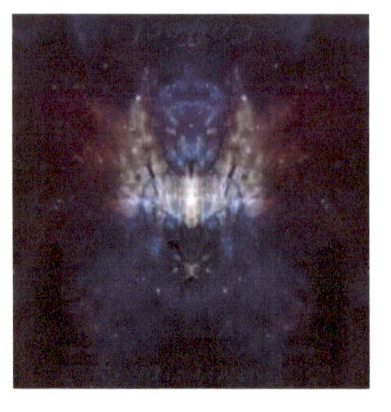

Collect

Insure

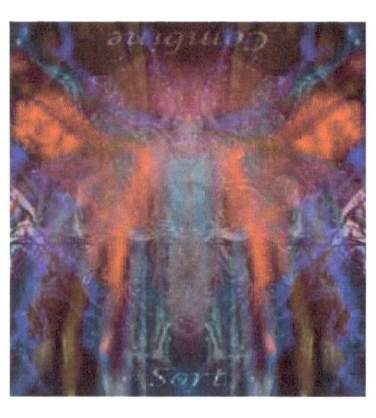

Combine

Sort

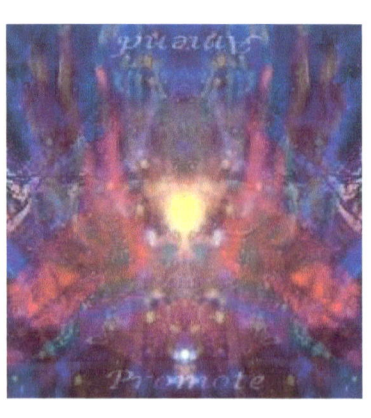

Amend

Promote

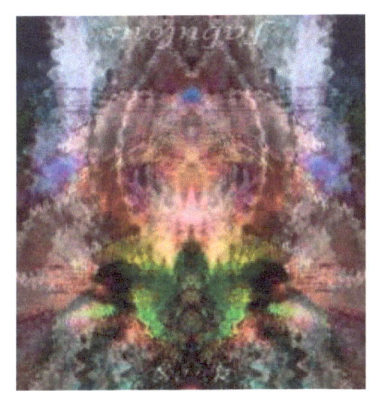

Fabulous
Seek

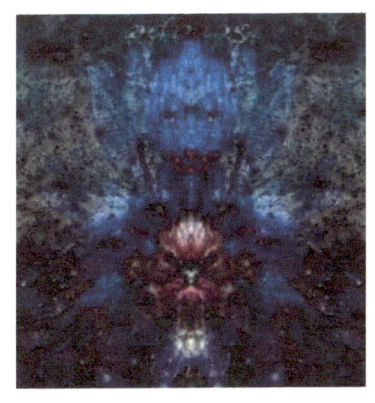

Scrape
Chat

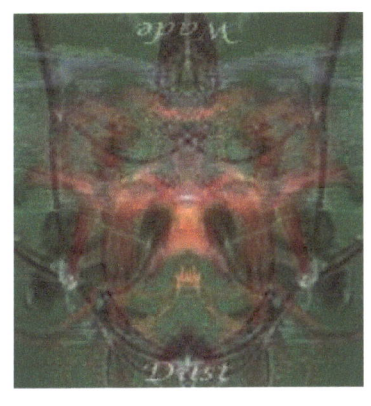

Wade
Dust

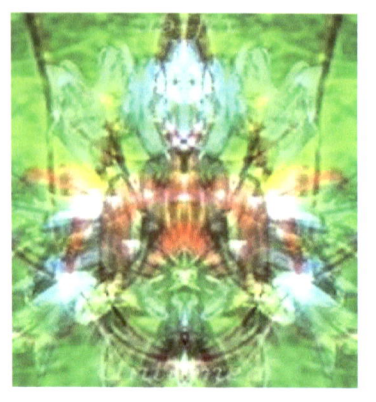

Offer
Untamed

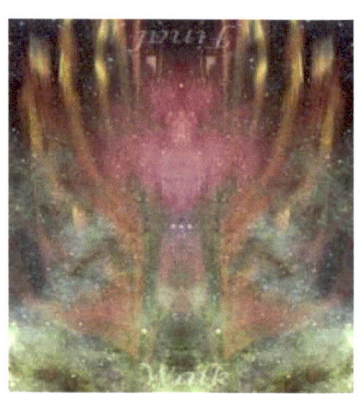

Final
Walk

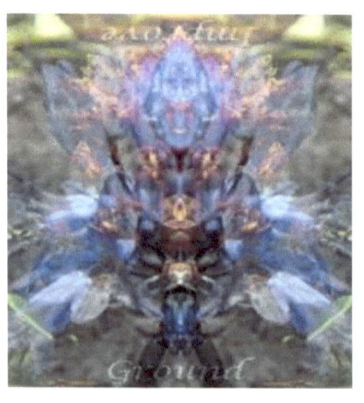

Improve
Ground

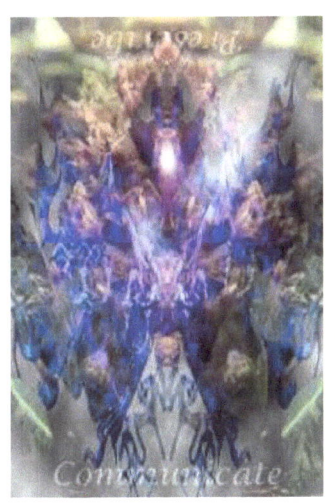

Prescribe

Communicate

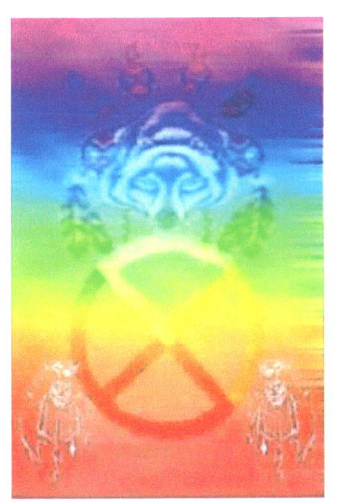

Wolf Rainbow

Medicine

www.ingramcontent.com/pod-product-compliance
Lightning Source LLC
Chambersburg PA
CBHW041618180526
45159CB00002BC/919